D0265132

Vincent van Gogh
The Troubled Artist

Anna Claybourne

HODDER
Wayland

an imprint of Hodder Children's Books

© 2003 White-Thomson Publishing Ltd

Produced by White-Thomson Publishing Ltd
2/3 St Andrew's Place, Lewes, BN7 1UP

Editor: Elaine Fuoco-Lang
Inside and cover design: Tim Mayer
Picture Research: Shelley Noronha –
    Glass Onion Pictures
Proofreader: Jane Colgan

Cover: A self-portrait by Vincent van Gogh painted in 1884.
Title page: A self-portrait by Vincent van Gogh painted
in 1886.

Published in Great Britain in 2003 by Hodder Wayland,
an imprint of Hodder Children's Books

Hodder Children's Books
An imprint of Hodder Headline Limited
338 Euston Road, London, NW1 3BH

British Library Cataloguing in Publication Data
Claybourne, Anna
    Van Gogh. - (Famous Lives)
    1. Gogh, Vincent van, 1853–1890 - Juvenile literature
    2. Painters - Netherlands - Biography - Juvenile
    literature
    I. Title
    750.9'492

ISBN 0 7502 4323 6

Printed in Hong Kong by Wing King Tong.

Picture acknowledgements:
AKG: cover and title page, 6, 9, 11, 14, 15, 18, 19, 21, 22,
23, 24, 26, 28, 29, 30, 31, 32, 34, 35, 38, 39, 44;
Bridgeman Art Library: 8, 21, 25, 33, 36, 40, 41;
Corbis: 42; Kröller-Müller Museum: 7; Popperfoto: 10, 17,
37; Topham: 4, 43, 45; Van Gogh Museum: 5, 16, 20, 27;
Yoke Matze: 12, 13, 16.

'How can I be useful, of what service can I be? There is something inside me, what can it be?'
Vincent expresses his longing to find his purpose in life in a letter to Theo.

However, as his letters to Theo show, he really wanted to be useful, but he had no idea how. He spent his time reading religious books and spent many hours thinking, but he couldn't discover what he wanted to do. He knew he had a purpose in life, but it would still take him years to find out that he wanted to be an artist.

This picture shows Paris in the 1880s. Vincent moved between Paris and London several times as a young man, and later went to live in Paris with Theo.

Searching for a Role

Vincent's next move, in April 1876, was to return to England to be a schoolteacher. He found work in a school in Ramsgate, Kent, where he taught French, German and maths. After a few months he moved to another job, which included some work as a Christian preacher. But he was still unsettled. By Christmas, he had left and was back home in Holland with his parents, who were now living in another village called Etten.

This modern-day photograph of Ramsgate (left) shows the same scene that van Gogh drew in 1876 (below).

A recent photograph of Amsterdam. In 1877 Vincent attended theological college in the city.

'Oh! might I be shown the way to devote my life more completely to the service of God and the Gospel'. From a letter to Theo, April 1877, when Vincent had decided he wanted to be a clergyman.

Vincent's family despaired over what would become of him. His mother knew how much he loved nature, and wished he could find a job in that area. His sister complained that his new-found interest in religion made him very dull. But Vincent felt that through his Christian beliefs, he could help people. After working for a short time in a bookshop, he finally decided to become a proper clergyman like his father. With his parents' help, he enrolled in theological college in Amsterdam in May 1877.

Vincent the Preacher

In Amsterdam Vincent had to study Latin and Greek, which he hated. He wanted to get on with the practical work of helping people, and couldn't see the point of learning old languages. After a year of struggling with his classes, he dropped out.

There was one last chance. His father took him to Brussels, where Vincent managed to complete a basic three-month course to become an evangelical preacher. At last, he found a temporary job in a town called Wasmes, in Belgium.

A typical scene in a square in Brussels at the end of the 19th century.

18

But Vincent's life as a clergyman went horribly wrong. He took himself far too seriously, giving away many of his clothes and living in a hut in an attempt to be like Jesus. He meant well, but the townspeople thought he was crazy. In July 1879, after just a few months, he was sacked for setting a bad example, and found himself unemployed yet again.

This is a coloured picture postcard of Brussels, taken in 1900, showing several old churches. Vincent tried a career in religion, but it turned out not to suit his character.

An Artist is Born

All this time Vincent had kept on drawing, making sketches of
his surroundings to send with his letters to his family. He had
always seen his drawing as just a hobby. In fact, when he was
in Brussels he had told Theo that he would like to draw more,
but shouldn't because it would keep him away from his work.

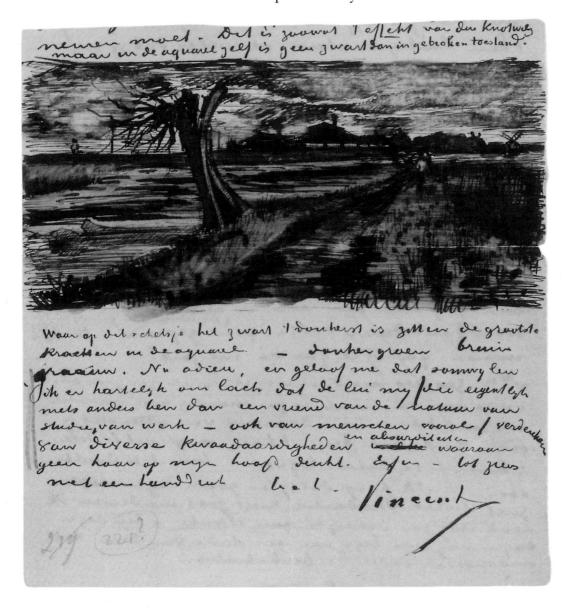

This letter from Vincent to Theo, written
on 17 September 1882, contains a sketch
of a countryside scene.

After being sacked from being a clergyman, Vincent stayed in Belgium for a while, but his interest in Christianity began to fade. Instead, he spent much of his time sketching the local miners on their way to work. He wrote to Theo asking him to send him prints of paintings by the old masters, and began teaching himself to paint by copying them. In the autumn of 1880, he moved back to Brussels, where he could take art lessons and visit galleries. Although no one knew it yet, at the age of 27, Vincent had discovered what he wanted to do. His real life had just begun.

This picture, called Women Miners, *is one of van Gogh's earliest paintings, dating from 1882.*

Vincent and Theo

Throughout their lives, Vincent and his younger brother Theo had been friends. But while Vincent had lost his way, searching desperately for his place in the world, Theo had stayed at Goupil & Co. and built up a solid career as an art dealer. He was now living in Paris. The brothers were not as close as they had once been, although they still exchanged letters.

Vincent painted this portrait of himself in 1884, when he was in his mid-thirties.

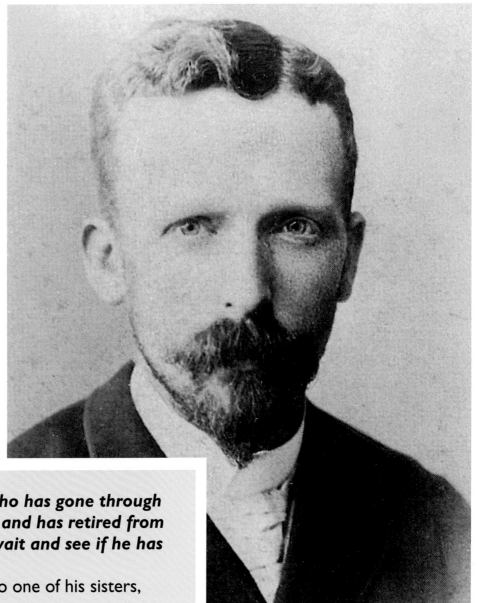

A photo of Theo van Gogh, taken in the late 1880s. Theo looked similar to his brother, but was smaller and thinner.

'Vincent is one of those who has gone through all the experiences of life and has retired from the world; now we must wait and see if he has genius. I think he has.'
Theo van Gogh in a letter to one of his sisters, October 1885.

But it was now that Theo came to Vincent's aid. He began to send him money to help buy the canvases and paints he needed for his new career, until Vincent could start to sell his paintings. Vincent often felt bad about accepting the money, but he came to rely on it. For the next ten years, Theo would support his older brother, however much it cost him and whatever sacrifices he had to make. His generosity, and his faith in Vincent's abilities, made Vincent's greatest works possible.

The Student Artist

Vincent loved to paint his surroundings and the countryside. He painted Farmhouses Among Trees *in September 1883 when he was living with his parents in Holland.*

Over the next few years, Vincent threw himself into perfecting his art. For much of the time, since money was short, he lived with his parents in southern Holland. By now, most of the family had given up on any hope of Vincent ever sticking to a proper job. But he worked hard, painting the countryside, local workers and rural buildings. He also went back to The Hague for a while, and there he began to sell some paintings to one of his art-dealer uncles. He was determined to devote all his strength to his art.

Many of Vincent's early paintings were studies of local people going about their everyday lives. This one, painted in 1882, is called **Scheveningen Women and Other People Under Umbrellas.**

'While painting, I feel of late a certain power of colour awakening in me, stronger and different from what I have felt till now.'
Letter to Theo,
August 1883.

Although Vincent was not yet painting the great pictures he is now remembered for, he was beginning to develop his unique style, with its thick lines, distorted shapes and strong colours. In 1884, Vincent and Theo made an agreement that Vincent would exchange his completed paintings for money from Theo. This made Vincent feel that he was earning Theo's money and not just taking it, and this allowed him to carry on working.

Unlucky in Love

Vincent often tried to have relationships, but they always went wrong. This was partly due to his eccentric and intense nature. He was always so serious, and had such strong feelings, that the girls he liked were often frightened away.

While living with his parents in Holland in 1881, Vincent fell head-over-heels in love with his widowed cousin Kee, who was staying there with her little boy. Vincent longed for a wife and family, and wanted to marry Kee, but his love was not returned.

A photo of Kee Vos and her son, taken in the early 1880s. Vincent fell in love with Kee and hoped the three of them would become a family, but it was not to be.

'I hope that he will find, some time, a wife who will love him so much that she will share his life, but it would be difficult to find one who would be fit for that.'
Theo despairs over Vincent's chances of love in a letter to his own wife Johanna.

Then, in The Hague the following year, Vincent lived with an unmarried mother called Sien. He spent all his money from Theo trying to support her and her children, until his family persuaded him to leave her.

At his parents' new house at Neunen, another romantic disaster took place. A neighbour named Margot fell in love with Vincent, and tried to kill herself when her family, who considered the unemployed artist deeply unsuitable, banned her from seeing him. Although he desperately longed for love, Vincent was never to have the companionship and support of a wife.

Van Gogh drew this picture of Sien sewing in 1883.

A Death in the Family

Vincent's father, Theodorus van Gogh. He died in March 1885, just before Vincent's 32nd birthday.

In 1885, Vincent was living with his parents at Neunen. He had rented a studio nearby, and was working hard, but his ageing parents were worried about him. In letters to relatives, his mother complained that Vincent was rude and difficult to live with, and said she thought he should spend more time with other artists. On 25 March, his father wrote that Vincent was depressed, and said he wished that things would start to go well for his son. Just two days later, Theodorus van Gogh went for a walk on the heath. When he returned, he collapsed at the front door and died.

The Potato Eaters, *painted just after the death of his father in 1885, is now considered to be van Gogh's first great painting.*

'It is not the language of painters but the language of nature which one should listen to.'
Vincent in a letter to Theo, written in 1882.

Vincent wrote to Theo that in the first few days after their father's death, he "could not work as usual". But soon afterwards he went to live in his studio and started to paint more than ever. Now that he wasn't living at home, he seemed to find a new freedom. That spring, he sent Theo a picture called *The Potato Eaters*. Today it is seen as the painting that marked the beginning of his career as a great artist.

Living with Theo

In early 1886, Vincent went to live with Theo in Paris. The brothers had discussed living together for some time, but Theo had told Vincent to wait until the summer, when he would be moving to a larger apartment. Vincent couldn't wait. With typical stubbornness, he turned up in Paris in February, without even warning Theo. That June, they moved together to a bigger place, with a bedroom each and a studio for Vincent.

In Paris, Vincent visited art galleries and increased his knowledge of the modern art scene. He met famous artists such as Pissarro, Degas and Monet, and made good friends with a younger artist, Emile Bernard.

Self-portrait with Dark Felt Hat, (left) was painted when Vincent was living with Theo in Paris in 1886.

But for Theo, living with his brother was a nightmare. Vincent was selfish, argumentative, messy and so obsessed with his work that he would talk about it late into the night. Theo could hardly get any sleep. But because he loved his brother so much and believed in his genius, Theo put up with this lifestyle for two years.

Vincent would have visited Parisian cafés like the one in this picture, **Woman in a Café**, painted by Edgar Degas in the late 19th century.

Vincent Heads South

Vincent loved Paris, and threw himself into painting the city scenery and people. But he soon yearned for the countryside again. He wanted to go to Provence, in the south of France, where it was warm and sunny. He dreamed of starting what he called a "Studio of the South": an artistic community where fellow artists could come and work with him and share ideas. Vincent especially wanted to invite an artist called Paul Gauguin, whom he admired deeply.

Vincent painted this self-portrait in 1887, shortly before he moved from Paris to Arles.

Vincent painted this countryside view of Arles, France, in 1888.

So in February 1888, he moved to Arles in Provence. Even though it was snowing when he arrived, Vincent had been right that the climate and colours of Provence would inspire him. That summer, he painted many of his most brilliant works, including *Sunflowers* and *Vincent's Bedroom at Arles*.

'I have a terrible lucidity at moments, when nature is so glorious. In those days I am hardly conscious of myself and the picture comes to me like in a dream ... Life is after all enchanting.'
Vincent describes his intensely creative state of mind in a letter to Theo, 1888.

But Vincent was pushing himself too hard. He lived in poverty, sometimes going without food so that he could buy paint with the money Theo sent him. He stayed up for days on end, working non-stop, obsessed with achieving perfection. He sometimes seemed to live in a kind of dream-world, having hallucinations and losing himself inside his own head.

The Ear Incident

Van Gogh's **Portrait of the Postman Roulin** *painted in 1888. This is a painting of one of the many local people Vincent made friends with in Arles. Despite his odd ways, Vincent always had loving friends who were willing to pose for portraits, and who looked after him in his times of need.*

Although his work was going brilliantly, Vincent was not well. He was overworked, half-starved, and so excited that he was on the verge of collapse. Towards the end of 1888, two things happened that finally pushed him over the edge.

Firstly, in October, Paul Gauguin agreed to come and work with Vincent at his studio in Arles. The two artists admired each other greatly, and during Gauguin's stay they inspired each other to paint many new works. However, they also annoyed each other and ended up having furious arguments, which added to Vincent's stress levels.

Then, in December, Theo announced that he was going to marry his girlfriend Johanna. This should have been good news but deep down Vincent knew it meant that he was no longer the only important person in Theo's life.

On 23 December, after another row, Gauguin stormed out of Vincent's house and went to stay in a hotel. Left alone, and very confused and upset, Vincent cut off part of his own left ear and went out into the streets with it. He was rescued by his friend Roulin, the postman, and ended up in hospital, where Theo went to stay with him over Christmas.

*This painting, **Self-Portrait with Bandaged Ear**, painted in 1889, shows Vincent after he had cut off part of his left ear.
The picture shows his right ear bandaged because Vincent looked in the mirror to paint it.*

In the Asylum

Theo went back to Paris, and Roulin the postman and
Reverend Salles, the local clergyman, looked after Vincent.
He seemed to recover well, but after leaving hospital, he was
plagued by more mental breakdowns. Some of his neighbours,
scared by his odd behaviour and clothes and his damaged ear,
started to complain. Although Vincent did not think he was
insane, he agreed to go into a mental asylum in nearby
St. Remy in May 1889.

This is one of the many paintings Vincent did of the asylum in St. Remy, where he stayed in 1889.

Since Vincent was not ill all the time, the sympathetic doctors let him roam freely and gave him a room to paint in.

He stayed at the asylum for a year, and painted some amazingly beautiful pictures, including *Irises*, *Cypresses* and *Starry Night*. But it was a time of painful suffering for him. Every few weeks, he endured attacks of unbearable panic, terror and despair.

'It was no longer the buoyant, sunny, triumphant work from Arles ... his palette has become more sober, the harmonies of his pictures have passed into a minor key.'
Johanna van Gogh-Bonger, describing the new work Vincent painted at the asylum.

Vincent van Gogh painted Starry Night in 1889 while he was in the St. Remy asylum. This photograph of people admiring the painting was taken at the grand opening of the Museum of Modern Art in Queens, New York, on 29 June 2002.

Was Vincent Insane?

The Absinthe Drinkers, *an 1876 painting by Edgar Degas. Absinthe was a very powerful alcoholic drink that could give people hallucinations. Many people drank it in 19th-century France, including Vincent.*

There have been many theories about what was wrong with Vincent van Gogh. Some think he suffered from depression, or that his breakdowns could have been caused by the stress of constantly starving and exhausting himself. He was also addicted to absinthe, a strong alcoholic drink that could cause hallucinations.

Some experts believe he may have had epilepsy, which could not be treated at that time. (Today, people with epilepsy can take medicine and do not suffer as much as they did during van Gogh's time.) He may also have had tinnitus, an unexplained ringing in the ears that has been known to drive people insane.

Whatever caused his problems, many people feel that van Gogh's intense experience of the world contributed to the brilliant vibrancy of his work.

In early 1890, Vincent appeared to recover. After a year at St. Remy, he went to visit Theo, Johanna and their new baby (named Vincent Willem after his uncle) and he seemed calm and healthy. Theo had arranged for him to live in Auvers-sur-Oise near Paris, where an old friend named Dr Gachet had agreed to keep an eye on him. Here, everyone hoped Vincent would be able to relax and focus on his painting.

Vincent's Portrait of Dr Gachet, painted in 1890. As well as being a doctor, Dr Gachet was a friend of many Paris artists and was deeply sympathetic to Vincent's problems. He was the perfect choice as a friend to watch over Vincent after he left the St. Remy asylum.

A Tragic Death

Vincent moved to Auvers-sur-Oise on 21 May 1890. He lodged at an inn, and spent his days painting and visiting Dr Gachet and his family. Friends from Paris came to see him, and Theo and Johanna hoped the worst was over. But these happy weeks at Auvers were to be Vincent's last.

On 27 July the owner of the inn where Vincent lived sent for Dr Gachet. The doctor found Vincent lying in bed with a bullet wound in his chest. He had gone to the fields to paint, and there he had taken out a gun and shot himself. He had managed to drag himself back to the inn, but was critically injured.

Wheat Fields with Crows, *painted in 1890, was one of Vincent's last paintings. It shows the kind of field in which he was working when he fatally shot himself.*

A note was immediately sent to Theo's workplace, but he only received it the next day. Theo rushed to Auvers-sur-Oise to be with Vincent. He hoped that his brother would survive, but Vincent said "This sadness will last forever ... I wish I could die now". That night, at 1.30 a.m., Vincent died in his brother's arms.

Many artists and friends came to the funeral. They surrounded Vincent's coffin with paintings and flowers, and he was buried in the cornfields. Theo was devastated.

'Well, my own work, I am risking my life for it and my reason has half-foundered owing to it ... what's the use?'
From one of Vincent's last letters to Theo, written in the summer of 1890.

A portrait of Vincent van Gogh on his deathbed, drawn on 29 July 1890 by his friend Dr Gachet.

The End for Theo

The loss of his beloved brother destroyed Theo. For over ten years he had sacrificed his own happiness, giving money to Vincent that he needed for himself and his family. He had put up with his brother's difficult behaviour so that Vincent could paint. Many times the brothers had said they functioned almost as one person. Together they had made the creation of Vincent's amazing paintings possible. Vincent had meant everything to Theo.

This statue of Vincent and Theo van Gogh stands in Groot Zundert in Holland, near Vincent's birthplace.

"par mon intermédiaire tu as ta part à la production même de certaines toiles qui même dans la débâcle gardent leur calme...

Vincent and Theo's graves in Auvers. At first Theo was buried in Utrecht, but later Johanna had him reburied next to his beloved brother. She had a sprig of ivy from Dr Gachet's garden planted there, and today it covers both the graves.

'It is a grief that will last and which I certainly shall never forget as long as I live ... Oh! mother, he was so my own, own brother!'
Theo grieves for Vincent in a letter to his mother, 1890.

Even though Theo adored his wife and his young son, he felt that life without Vincent had lost its meaning. Weakened by grief, he became ill and died just six months after his brother. His devoted wife Johanna eventually had him buried next to Vincent in Auvers.

Fame at Last

After Vincent and Theo died, Johanna van Gogh-Bonger, Theo's wife, committed herself to preserving Vincent's paintings. She also collected and catalogued the brothers' letters, and wrote a personal memoir of Vincent's life. Through her work, his art became better known, and people started to buy it. By the early 1900s, the art world was aware of Vincent's genius, and he became a major influence on other artists throughout the 20th century.

Theo's wife, Johanna van Gogh-Bonger, with their son in a photograph taken in 1890.

'Happiness ... it lies in the joy of achievement, in the thrill of creative effort.'
Vincent in a letter to Theo. This quotation shows that although he never won wide recognition in his own lifetime, Vincent found fulfilment in creating his art and knew it was the right thing for him to do.

The world's biggest collection of van Gogh's paintings is at the Rijksmuseum Vincent van Gogh in Amsterdam.

In 1960, several surviving members of the van Gogh family, including Theo's son Vincent Willem van Gogh, founded the Vincent van Gogh Foundation to protect and collect his work. In 1973, the foundation opened the Rijksmuseum Vincent van Gogh (Vincent van Gogh museum) in Amsterdam.

Today, Vincent van Gogh is one of the world's most popular artists, and his paintings regularly sell for many millions of pounds. His belief in his work, and Theo's belief in him, had been right all along.

Glossary

Absinthe A very strong alcoholic drink popular in 19th-century France.

Aloof Uninterested, distant or snobbish.

Asylum A hospital or home for mentally ill people.

Auction A sale of art, antiques or other items in which the buyers make bids.

Auctioneers A company that arranges auctions.

Bookbinder Someone who makes books.

Canvas A sheet of thick fabric stretched over a frame for painting on.

Cataloguing Making a complete list of an artist's known work.

Clergyman A priest or vicar.

Community A group or society.

Depression A mental illness that makes people feel sad and hopeless.

Eccentric An eccentric person is someone who behaves oddly and doesn't fit in.

Enroll To be registered as a student.

Epilepsy A disease that affects the brain.

Evangelical A kind of Christianity based on a literal belief in the Bible.

Hallucination A vision of something that is not really there.

Lucidity The ability to think and understand things clearly.

Memoir A collection of personal memories.

Mental To do with the mind.

Minor key In music, this means a musical scale that has a sad sound. It can also be used as a metaphor for sad or muted colours in paintings.

Obstinate Stubborn and strong-minded.

Old masters Great artists from the past.

Palette A selection of colours.

Rural To do with the countryside.

Solitary Alone, or preferring to be alone.

Suburb An outlying area of a city.

Theological college A university where people study to be priests.

Tinnitus Unexplained ringing in the ears.

Further Information

Sources

The Letters of Vincent van Gogh edited by Mark Roskill (Flamingo, 2000)

Van Gogh by Melissa McQuillan (Thames and Hudson, 1989)

Books

My Sticker Art Gallery – Van Gogh by Carole Armstrong (Frances Lincoln, 1996)

The Life and Work of Vincent van Gogh by Sean Connolly (Heinemann Library, 2000)

An Introducion to Art: Van Gogh by Peter Harrison (Hodder Wayland, 2001)

Tell Me About van Gogh by John Malam (Evans Brothers, 1996)

Vincent van Gogh (Artists in their time) by Ruth Thomson (Franklin Watts, 2002)

Date Chart

1853, 30 March Vincent van Gogh born in Zundert, Holland.

1857, 1 May Birth of Vincent's favourite brother, Theo.

1865-1869 Vincent goes to boarding school.

1869, July Starts work as a trainee art dealer at Goupil & Co. in The Hague.

1873, June Moves to London, to work in Goupil's offices there.

1874, Spring Suffers his first romantic rejection and becomes withdrawn.

1874, October Moves to Goupil's offices in Paris.

1874, December Is sent back to London.

1875, May Is sent back to Paris again.

1876, January Goupil & Co. give Vincent three months' notice to leave.

1876, April Goes to work as a teacher in Ramsgate and Isleworth in England, and starts working as a lay (untrained) preacher.

1876, December Goes to stay with his family in Holland and decides not to return to England.

1877, January Starts work in a bookshop in Dordrecht, Holland.

1877, May Goes to Amsterdam to train to be a priest.

1878, July Gives up his training and goes to Brussels to train as an evangelical preacher instead.

1879, January Gets his first job as a clergyman in Wasmes, Belgium, but is sacked after a few months.

1880, July Makes a decision to study art.

1880, October Goes to Brussels and begins art lessons.

1881, April Returns to Holland to live with his parents.

1881, December Goes to live in The Hague to take art lessons there.

1883, December Returns to live with his parents in Neunen.

1885, 25 March Death of Vincent's father, Theodorus van Gogh.

1885, November Moves to Antwerp.

1886, February Goes to live with his brother Theo in Paris.

1888, February Moves to Arles in the south of France.

1888, 23 December Cuts off his own ear while suffering from mental illness.

1889, 8 May Goes to live in a mental asylum at St. Remy, near Arles.

1890, 16 May Goes to visit Theo, his wife Johanna and their new baby son in Paris.

1890, 21 May Moves to Auvers-sur-Oise near Paris.

1890, 27 July Shoots himself while out painting in the cornfields in Auvers-sur-Oise, and dies two days later.

1891, 25 January Theo dies of a combination of illnesses made worse by his grief.

Index

All numbers in **bold** refer to pictures as well as text.